# Shatter

April Harold

Presentation by *BookLeaf Publishing*

Web: www.bookleafpub.com

E-mail: info@bookleafpub.com

ISBN: 9789357440134

First edition 2023

# DEDICATION

For A.  Because I promised you I would.

# Arm's Length

1

I don't dictate my thoughts. Never have.

I write. Type. Jot. Transcribe.

I will not speak them with my voice.

They are safer on the page at arm's length,
outside of my head and heart.

They do less damage there.

# Articulate

2

You were the one

Who captured my heart in your hands

I lost you

Because I didn't know how to say

"I love you, please choose me"

# Regret

What were you thinking?

On the phone. Same as so many times before, but this time, different.

His voice in your ear; your voice in his head. Promises; temptations. Longing so visceral, you could almost see him walk through your door.

It was what you both wanted. Adults can make their own decisions. Your entire being was screaming for you to let it happen.

And you said no.

You chose, instead, to be loyal. To the one who never even considered being loyal to you. To the one who made you shrink, made you small, made you doubt yourself.

His voice, on the phone, reminded you that you were worthy. You were powerful. You were the queen of your own body and soul and heart. His voice made you want to live in the most match-struck way possible.

And you said no.

Who might you have turned out to be, if you had just said yes?

Regret never leaves us; not really.

# Anorexic Love

Skinny love. Anorexic love. Absent love. All of
the above.

I gave you all of me; my body, my time, my
heart, my loyalty. What the fuck was it for?

I chipped and sliced and shoved down all the
brilliant parts of myself trying to find the one
shiny piece I was convinced would win me your
love.

I never found it. I believed for so long that it
didn't exist. Therefore, neither did I.

But you took and took and swallowed me whole.
And I let you because I was starving for one
shred of validation.

Until I wasn't.

You were clueless, and greedy, and chicken shit.
You never deserved me in the first place.

Give me my eight god damn years back.

# Shatter

It started like an ember. A warmth spreading like
whiskey through my chest with amber heat.

Voices wove their way through my head;
pinpricks of light bursting through the darkness.

Hearts like soft glass, shimmers spiraling
upward; now shattered across the expanse.

Not all glass is recyclable, after all.

# Rescue

I thought I needed rescue

That I needed a savior for my heart

And you were so very willing to play the role

White Knight on his steed

"Always on guard, my princess"

Only I didn't realize that rescue was your calling

Your currency; your self-worth

That it wasn't me you were rescuing

It was just your attempt to rescue your own
wounds

The ones you don't even know are there

Pity, you can't even save yourself

Lord knows, you didn't save me

# Run

The first time they lie to your face.

Run.

The moment they say you're not good enough.

Run.

When the eyes staring back at you turn hollow.

Run.

When the voices are nagging, the sadness is screaming, and truth is hammering hard at your door.

When you realize that you have the power to save yourself.

RUN.

# Forty

I was heartbroken.  Anxious.  In pain.

I was alone.  Inside a marriage, alone.

It was my fortieth birthday.

It was the day I decided my marriage was no longer worth saving.

It was the day I decided I to save myself.

# Tilting

And he stands at the top of the windmill

Peering down at all those who never gave him
the credit he so desperately felt he was due

Never realizing he's been chasing that
recognition forever

Long since the shadow was created by the Sun

# Tomorrow

"It will all be better tomorrow."

It was always so easy for you to deflect.

Sweep it under the rug.  Move right past it.

As if we don't ever need to talk about it again.

But it didn't work, did it?

Our issues didn't just magically disappear the next day.

As if our lives were never touched or blemished or crumbling.

And you wonder why the cracks that you thought were so small became big and large and giant.

Until, suddenly, the foundation was so deteriorated that there was no way to repair it ever again.

# Quiet

Quiet. It is a new experience, here in this small little house. Quiet. No singing, no chatter, no laughter or complaints or "mom!" from across the hall. Just quiet.

These last three weeks are the longest we've ever been apart. Coming up on 11 years, and I've been present for almost every single day. And now, quiet.

Divorce is hard. It's messy, draining, humbling, shameful, liberating, and upending all at once. Dividing pennies, possessions, and plans. Laying out a road map for where we are hoping to get in the future, though we now have so much less clarity on how to get there.

Dismantling a life is difficult enough; but how do you share a being? Parse out the moments you cling to while calendaring your time together and apart? Watching the days spread into weeks, into months. Knowing you should be savoring the uniqueness of space, but unable to fill the empty shadow with anything but the memory of a shimmering sound.

It's consistently baffling. I don't think I'll ever get used to it. The quiet.

# Imperfection

12

I have an imperfect body.

I am an imperfect mother.

It will be okay, I tell myself.

It will be okay.

# Would Have

13

For 30 years my body knew how to prime. Why would it forget now?

There is no longer a source; surgical precision.

But every month it tries.

Oil. Irritation. Blemish. It still thinks it can bleed.

Should have gotten pregnant.

Could have had another.

Would have, I think to myself; would have.

# It's Happening

It's happening.

The enticement. The one-ups-man-ship.

The party parent vs. the one that takes care of all
the necessary, mundane, life-related boring
things.

I chose security, for her.

I chose a place where we could compromise,
before you fled.

I chose a garden and quiet and structure and a
park and so many other vitally important things.

And here you go with your flash and fun and
rule-less world.

It's happening already.

# Feral

15

I had been having this feeling for weeks.

While my child was not with me because he wouldn't send her home.

When I had no idea how to get her back to where she belonged, and didn't know if I ever would.

A mother's panic. Desperation.

Clawing at something so unforgiving only to have it rob you of all your strength, and still not give you what you needed.

Fight or flight.

Feral.

Fear.

# Free Will

I have been working, oh so hard. Emotions are complicated things, you see, and I have so many of them.

Betrayal for the fact that you poisoned what was left. Fear at the thought of losing my most precious gift. Anger at the way you so deftly twist my words. Desperation at the need to make you pay.

You deserve to suffer for what you've done. You deserve to be held accountable for the pain you have caused. You deserve to be made to own up to your responsibilities; every single one.

But that is a deep dark hole of ilk and negativity and I will not let you drag me into it. None of it will get me to my goal; what is best for her, what is best for me.

I will keep doing the hard work. I can overcome the hatred. I am more powerful than your betrayal. It is a choice to walk into the light.

Free will is a beautiful thing.

# Heartbreak



The size of my heartbreak is filling this house.

It started by filling my bed at night when
everything was quiet.

Then it filled up the whole room.

Then it spilled over through the hallway into the
room that used to be yours and all its silence.

And now it has filled every space in here.

I carry it with me every day.

# Careless

You are careless.

Careless with our most precious gift.

Willing to let go the reigns to whomever should cross your path, as long as it will lighten your burden.

Parenting is oh, so hard, after all.

I wonder how old they will be when they realize you were careless with their heart.

Just like you were careless with mine.

# Hollow

19

There's a hollow in my chest where memories of you live

Sometimes they're more towards the surface, and sometimes they're farther down

And sometimes I miss you so badly that hollow turns into a black hole

It takes every ounce of my being to pretend it's not there

Because if I don't, and I fall in, it will swallow me whole

And I might never get back out

# As If

You assume this decision was easy for me

As if I stood by with glee while watching my world burn

Knowing that, simultaneously, I was also burning yours

But I had a life to resurrect, and a child to raise

Trust me, my pyre of heartbreak was there every day

Just not bright enough for you to see

# I Will

I have disappeared. It was not sudden.

I have spent years of my life trying to be someone I am not.

I shut off all the pieces of myself that made me true.

I became raw, and ran towards my damaged parts to cover and protect them.

I am trying to find my way back to my soul.

I am still healing. I am still learning. I am working my way back up.

I will get there, I think.

I will not get there, I fear.

I will put one foot in front of the other.

Every god damn day.

www.ingramcontent.com/pod-product-compliance
Lightning Source LLC
LaVergne TN
LVHW050307200726
843509LV00015B/3208